Picture Perfect

by Lisa Trumbauer

STECK-VAUGHN
Harcourt Supplemental Publishers

www.steck-vaughn.com

Do you remember when everyone in your class had a photograph taken for school? Everyone lined up in front of a camera. A **photographer** told you where to stand so that everyone's face would be seen.

Then the photographer probably asked you
to look into the camera, smile, and say "Cheese!"
Pushing a button, the photographer took a photograph.
CLICK! You and your class looked picture perfect!

Have you ever tried taking a photograph? Taking photos is called **photography.** In order to take photos, you need a camera. You also need to know how a camera works.

Pressing this button opens the **shutter** inside the camera. The shutter opens and closes very quickly. It lets light into the camera.

Film goes inside the camera. The film stores the image for a photo.

The part of the camera that you look through is called a **viewfinder.**

This is the **lens.**
A lens is a curved piece of glass or plastic.

To take a photo, look through the viewfinder. If you like what you see, push the button on the top of the camera. This button opens the shutter.

Light passes through the shutter in less than
a second. It lands on the film inside the camera.
The light records the image you see onto the film.

Some kinds of cameras don't need film. **Digital cameras** have a tiny computer inside. The computer stores the image you take. You can see the image you took right on the camera. Then you can print your own photos using a home computer.

Photos from film cameras are printed in a different way. The film inside the camera must be **developed** by treating it with special chemicals. The chemicals turn the film into negatives. A **negative** is like an opposite picture of the photo. Light colors look dark, and dark colors look light.

negative

photo

Negatives are used to print photographs. A special machine is used to shine light through the negatives onto special paper. The light records the image taken with the camera on the paper. The special paper becomes a photograph!

Today, taking a picture is as easy as one, two, three! Often, all you have to do is push a button. Special stores print photos from film in a very short time. The photos may be color, or they may be black and white.

Taking photos wasn't always as easy as it is today. People had to learn how to make photography work. They tried using light. They tried using different kinds of cameras.

The first cameras were very big and heavy. They did not use film. They used big metal plates. Chemicals were spread over the metal. The chemicals recorded the image on the metal plate.

13

It took a lot of time for the chemical to record the image. So people had to sit still for many minutes. They could not move or the picture would not be clear. Do you think that your whole class could sit still for fifteen minutes?

Also, these early cameras only took one picture at a time. Each metal plate held only one picture. Photographers had to remove the plate after taking each picture. These cameras only took pictures in black and white.

People continued to work with photography. In time, pictures could be taken more quickly. People said they were taken in a "snap," like the time it takes to snap your fingers. These kinds of photos were called **snapshots.**

People began finding ways to make cameras better.
They added new parts. Film took the place of the
metal plates. But cameras were still big and heavy.

In 1888, a man named George Eastman made a new kind of camera. It was small enough to fit in a person's hand. His camera held film for 100 pictures. Once all the pictures were taken, the photographer sent the camera back to Eastman.

MR. EASTMAN IN 1890

Eastman had also found an easier way to print photos from film. He built a factory. People in his factory printed photos from the film in the camera. Then they mailed back the camera with the printed photos. They even sent new film, too.

Cameras kept getting better. People wanted to take photos even when there was little light. So in the 1930s, **flashbulbs** were invented. In the 1940s, a new kind of film was made. The new color film meant that photos could be made in color.

In 1948, the first **instant cameras** were sold in stores. With an instant camera, people could take a photograph and it would slide out of the camera right away.

Digital cameras are a newer kind of instant camera. These cameras don't use film at all. Computers are used to store and print digital photos.

Cameras Through the Years

1839

Cameras were an amazing invention. For the first time, people were able to record exact images of people, places, and things for other people to see. So hold still and say, "Cheese!" CLICK! You're picture perfect!

Courtesy George Eastman House

1888

1949

1977

1986

2003

Glossary

camera	a machine used to take a photograph
developed	treated with chemicals so that an image can be seen
digital cameras	cameras that use a computer to store images
film	material on which images are recorded in a camera
flashbulbs	bright light bulbs that are used for taking photographs
instant cameras	cameras that make photos right away
lens	a curved piece of glass or plastic
negative	the developed film used to print photographs
photographer	someone who takes photographs
photography	the process of taking pictures with a camera
shutter	the part of a camera that opens to let in light
snapshots	photographs that can be taken quickly
viewfinder	the part of a camera that a photographer looks through